For Mom & Dad
Thank you for allowing my love of the game to grow unbiased, and helping me find the importance in my own controllables.

Contents

Introduction..........................	i
Understanding Mental Toughness........................	03
Developing Resilience...............	06
Building Mental Toughness.........	13
Your 3 Controllables..................	21
I Embrace the Uncertainty..........	31
Mountains to Molehills..............	34
The 2 States of Being................	37
Achieving Victory with a Winning Mindset.................................	41
Solidifying Your Foundation........	44
Further Resources....................	46

Pro Tip From Coach Austin:
"Throughout this guide, you'll see notes from me with tips to begin applying the techniques discussed."

Introduction

In the high-pressure position of goaltending, success isn't only found through physical skill level—it's found in mental fortitude. The ability to remain composed under pressure, bounce back from setbacks, and maintain focus amidst chaos can often be the defining factor between victory and defeat. This is where mental toughness and resilience come into play.

This book delves into the critical role that mental toughness and resilience play in the performance of hockey goaltenders. It explores how these intangible qualities can elevate a goaltender's game and set them apart from their competitors, regardless of their level of talent. Throughout the pages of this short guide, you will discover practical strategies and techniques to develop and strengthen your mental skills, empowering you to perform at your peak when it matters most.

From understanding the fundamentals of mental toughness to learning how to overcome adversity and cultivate a winning mindset, this book covers a wide range of topics essential for goaltenders looking to enhance their mental game. Through real-life examples, and actionable steps, you will gain the tools you need to not only hit your goals, but to go beyond them in the demanding world of ice hockey goaltending.

Whether you're a seasoned veteran or a novice goaltender, this guide is a roadmap to unlocking the secrets of mental toughness and resilience. Get ready to transform your game and emerge as a goaltender who not only stops pucks, but dominates the game with unwavering mental strength!

As someone who has personally struggled with anxiety in the net, I know the impact it can have on an athlete's performance.

For years, I battled self-doubt and anxiety, which often held me back. Despite the daunting odds and the naysayers who doubted my abilities, I sought to persevere. Transitioning from high school to an NCAA hockey team seemed like an insurmountable challenge, and unheard of in today's hockey world, but I refused to let fear of failure deter me. Instead, I embraced the adversity, using it as fuel to propel myself forward. Through grit and resilience, I defied the odds and earned my place on a D2 NCAA college hockey team.

My journey through my playing career and into the realm of coaching has taught me the invaluable lesson that mental toughness isn't something you're born with, you can train it and build it.

Having experienced the transformative power of mental fortitude, I am deeply aware of its profound impact. I am enthusiastic about imparting the strategies and techniques that have propelled me forward in my life to those who seek to embark on a similar journey of self-discovery and achievement.

Thank you for taking the next step on this journey.
Let's get started!

COACH AUSTIN CHRISTOPHER
THE MENTAL GOALIE

CHAPTER 1

UNDERSTANDING MENTAL TOUGHNESS

Mental toughness is often spoken about in athletics, and it's been coined many times by former marines and veterans that reflect back on their service. If you are familiar with the work of David Goggins, then you know what I'm talking about! It's important to understand the full definition of mental toughness in regards to goaltending and how building it will help your confidence, performance, and attitude.

Mental toughness encompasses the ability to maintain focus, composure, and resilience in the face of adversity. For athletes, it goes beyond mere physical skill; it is the unwavering resolve to perform at one's best, regardless of external pressures or challenges. In essence, being mentally tough is the ability to block out external forces, ignore internal doubts, and powerfully focus on the task at hand. Mental toughness enables the best athletes in the world to thrive in high-pressure situations. And as a goalie, high pressure situations are a given.

In goaltending, where split-second decisions and lightning-fast reactions can make all the difference, mental toughness serves as a catalyst for success. It empowers goaltenders to ride the ups and downs of competition with grace and determination, like a surfer that refuses to get thrown by tumultuous waves. By relying on internal drive and thick skin, goaltenders can maintain peak performance levels even in the face of external adversity.

What does a mentally tough goalie look like?
Mentally tough goaltenders exhibit a unique set of characteristics that distinguish them on and off the ice. They possess an unshakeable self-belief and confidence in their abilities, allowing them to approach each game with consistent determination. Often, mentally tough athletes 'Embrace the Uncertainty', a phrase we will dive into later, understanding that they cannot predict every outcome that is available. Instead, they accept the unknown, allowing the fear of failure and worry to leave their minds.

Resilience is another hallmark trait, as mentally tough goaltenders can bounce back quickly from setbacks, using failure as a stepping stone to future success. Think of your favorite NHL goalie. Besides the odd 5-6 goal game, NHL goalies do an incredible job of shaking off a goal and still performing at the top of their game afterward. Are you able to say the same about your game?

Resilience isn't only applicable to in-game scenarios. A mentally tough athlete is going to bounce back from bad seasons, trades, getting cut, injuries, bad coaching relationships, and negative naysayers quickly. They don't allow external whims to interrupt their internal chatter.

Additionally, a mentally tough goalie demonstrates exceptional focus and concentration, maintaining their composure even in the most chaotic of situations on the ice. They possess a strong sense of adaptability and are able to adjust their mindset and strategy as needed to overcome challenges and obstacles.

Understanding mental toughness is essential for goaltenders seeking to elevate their game to new heights. By embracing the defining characteristics of mental toughness and recognizing its pivotal role in sports performance, you can begin to cultivate the resilience, confidence, and determination needed to develop a strong mind and thick skin on the ice.

Pro Tip From Coach Austin:
"After finishing this chapter, take a moment to reflect back on the best goalies you've ever seen play. NHL, college, world juniors...etc. Remember instances when they gave up goals, or got pulled in a game. Remember how they bounced back afterward. What are some areas in your game that you know you could improve your mental strength in?"

CHAPTER 2

DEVELOPING RESILIENCE

Resilience is the bedrock upon which mental toughness is built, serving as a critical attribute for goaltenders striving for success on the ice. Being resilient means you are able to bounce back from setbacks, stare down adversity, and ultimately emerge stronger and more determined through every obstacle.

In the realm of sports, look at the many tales of athletes that have defied the odds, overcoming seemingly insurmountable challenges to achieve greatness. The story of Michael Jordan always pops into my mind. Cut from his high school basketball team, he goes on to be the greatest basketball player of all time.

In the NHL, look at elite Vegas Golden Knights goaltender Logan Thompson. After playing for the WHL's Brandon Wheat Kings, Thompson joined the Canadian university league in 2018-19 at Brock University. Getting to the NHL from a Canadian university is almost unheard of in today's game. Thompson persevered, and even after making it to the show, had to deal with plenty of critics and external pressure telling him he wasn't good enough. Now, he's an essential part of a great Golden Knights' club.

Even a guy like Marc-Andre Fleury, one the NHL's all time greats, has had adversity to face in his career. In the prime of his career, he was, unprotected by Pittsburg in the Vegas expansion draft. Pittsburg put their faith into a much younger Matt Murray at the time. Murray proved to be a bust for Pittsburg, while Fleury carried Vegas to the Stanley Cup final in his first season with them.

Tim Thomas is yet another example of a goalie that had every obstacle thrown in front of him and defied all odds as he rose from a ninth-round pick in the 1994 NHL Entry Draft to become one of the league's top goaltenders. After college hockey at the University of Vermont, he was tossed around in the minors before going overseas to finish his career, or so he thought. Boston signed and brought Thomas back to America, but he stayed in Providence, waiting years to earn an NHL role. Despite his unconventional style, and age, Thomas earned the starting role in Boston, won the Vezina Trophy twice, the second time at 37 years old, the the oldest goalie to ever win it. In 2011, he led the Boston Bruins to the Stanley Cup, claiming the Conn Smythe Trophy as playoff MVP. Mental toughness and resilience was a powerful factor through Thomas's career, and in the early 2010's, he even had an apparel line call "PPW", a.k.a. Prove People Wrong. He certainly did that, and his story is an inspiration to all goalies!

Everywhere there are examples of athletes dealing with pressure and setbacks externally, but still rising above. One of my favorite quotes about resilience came from the incredible Gordie Howe. He said:

"You've got to love what you're doing. If you love it, you can overcome any handicap or the soreness or all the aches and pains, and continue to play for a long, long time." - Gordie Howe

Howe had a career that stretched over 5 decades, and is considered one of the greatest hockey players of all time. If that quote doesn't represent resilience, I don't know what does. These stories serve as powerful reminders of the transformative power of resilience and the indomitable mindset that being mentally tough provides.

📌 **Pro Tip From Coach Austin:**
"Research some of your favorite professional athletes. Where did they experience adversity in their careers and overcame obstacles to be at the top of their game?

You'll find almost every elite athlete you look up to had to overcome adversity and setbacks along their career journey."

Understanding Resilience and Its Significance for Goaltenders:

Resilience is not merely about bouncing back from failure; it is about embracing failure as an opportunity for growth and learning. For goaltenders, resilience is synonymous with mental toughness, as it enables them to weather the inevitable storms of competition with acceptance and determination. Understanding resilience involves recognizing that setbacks are not permanent, but rather temporary roadblocks on the path to success. It requires a shift in perspective, viewing challenges as opportunities for self-improvement rather than insurmountable obstacles.

What are some obstacles we encounter every season?
- Losing Streak: We can sometimes face periods where we struggle to find our form, leading to a string of losses. While this can be disheartening, it presents an opportunity for a mentally tough goaltender to refine their technique and bounce back. By viewing a losing streak as a chance to learn and grow, goalies can emerge from it stronger and more prepared to face challenges in the future. By viewing every new day as an opportunity to snap the streak, we are no longer focused on the past, but instead, the present.
- Being Benched: Being benched can bruise our ego and confidence, but we can try and view as an opportunity for self-reflection and motivation. Instead of dwelling on feelings of disappointment or frustration, we will use this time to double our effort in practice, and prove to ourselves worthy of reclaiming the net. A mentally tough goalie will view being benched as a temporary setback rather than a permanent failure, and they will still show up everyday as if they are the starter, even when they are struggling to earn the net.

- Injury: When we face an injury, it can be devastating, especially if we are sidelined for a significant period. However, instead of viewing it as a setback, we can view it as an opportunity to focus on other aspects of our game, such as mental training, strategy analysis, or strengthening our weaker areas. To a mentally strong athlete, this time off the ice can provide an opportunity for introspection and growth, ultimately making a more well-rounded and resilient athlete when they return.
- Goals Against: A goal against is challenging as well, as it represents a breakdown of our primary objective of stopping pucks. However, what is the one thing we know for certain as a goalie? We will get scored on! Rather than dwelling on the negative outcome, we can view a goal as an opportunity. Number one, it can serve as a reminder of the importance of resilience and mental fortitude, motivating us to bounce back stronger and more focused for the remainder of the game. Number two, knowing that if we dwell on it right now, we won't be able to play our best. A goal against can help you return to the present moment and focus on the task at hand.

Pro Tip From Coach Austin:

"When dealing with goals against and other similar setbacks, our brains like to analyze them right away. This is great for work and school, but is not good for the middle of a hockey game! In these moments, I tell myself "I will think about this later". Saying this releases my mind from the goal because I am promising myself that I will go over the mistake in-depth at another time. This satisfies me for the moment, and let's me shift to the next play."

Strategies for Bouncing Back from Setbacks:
- Embrace Failure as a Learning Opportunity:
    - Reframe setbacks as opportunities for growth and learning. Know that you are always growing.
    - Analyze mistakes without dwelling on them, focusing instead on actionable takeaways for improvement. Tell yourself "I will think about this goal later".
- Develop a Growth Mindset:
    - Cultivate a mindset that sees challenges as opportunities rather than obstacles. Falling down is an opportunity to get back up.
    - Embrace setbacks as part of the journey towards excellence. Failure is not final but a stepping stone to success.
- Practice Self-Compassion:
    - Treat yourself with kindness and understanding, especially in moments of disappointment or defeat.
    - Acknowledge your efforts and progress, regardless of the outcome, to foster a sense of self-worth independent of performance.

Techniques for Maintaining Focus During Challenging Situations:
- Visualization:
    - Visualize successful outcomes, saves, situations, and positive scenarios, reinforcing confidence and self-belief.
    - Use mental imagery to simulate challenging situations and see yourself maintaining focus and composure under pressure.
- Mindfulness Meditation:
    - Use mindfulness techniques, such as deep breathing and emotion scans, to keep thoughts and emotions grounded and centered during games and practices.

- Self check: Ask yourself if you're being resilient and focusing on what you can do or if you're being affected by external factors.
- Positive Self-Talk:
    - Develop a repertoire of positive affirmations and self-talk phrases to counter negative thoughts and bolster confidence.
    - Challenge self-limiting beliefs and replace them with empowering, affirming statements that reinforce resilience and mental toughness.
    - "I am tough. I am confident. I am strong. I am where I am supposed to be. I embrace the uncertainty. I accept the unexpected."

Pro Tip From Coach Austin:
"Check out my confidence guide 'Stop Doubting & Start Dominating! A Goaltenders' Guide to Building Confidence in the Crease' to develop personal affirmations to help your resilience. Use the QR code here for a copy."

Being resilient also means accepting that not everything is going to go your way on the ice. There will be goals scored, mistakes made, and tough games lost. But it's how you respond to these challenges that defines you as a goalie. The one thing we know for certain as a goalie is that we will get scored on. Maybe it's not today, maybe not even tomorrow, but without a doubt, at some point we will give up a goal (or more than a goal!). The best goalies in the world are not immune to giving up goals, their power and skill lies in knowing how to bounce back when they do.

Once you can accept that not everything will go as you'd like on the ice, only then can you begin to build mental resilience and toughness. That's the mindset of a true goalie.

CHAPTER 3

BUILDING MENTAL TOUGHNESS

Throughout my journey as a player and coach, I've come to a profound realization: mental toughness is a skill that can be developed and honed over time. It's not something reserved for those who have endured extreme hardships in their past; rather, it's a quality that anyone can cultivate with the right training and mindset. While it's true that individuals who have faced significant challenges may have had the opportunity to strengthen their mental resilience, it's equally important to recognize that adversity comes in many forms. Whether you've faced hardships or not, the path to mental toughness lies in consistent practice, self-awareness, and a willingness to push beyond your comfort zone.

Similar to resilience, mental toughness entails reacting consistently regardless of whether the outcome is favorable or unfavorable. Consider the scenario of conceding a goal versus your team scoring one. Unless it's the final moments of the game, there's still time remaining. A mentally tough goalie maintains the same response whether they've just been scored on or their team has scored. This mindset is cultivated through recognizing that each moment on the ice presents an opportunity for action, and maintaining composure and focus, regardless of the circumstances, is key to success.

If you allow yourself to be swept up in the emotions of a goal against, or even a goal for, you are losing control of your mind, and therefore, your mental composure. Regardless of the score, your responsibilities as a goaltender remain the same: Stop the puck. A mentally tough athlete understands this, and maintains a consistent mindset throughout the game, reacting in a composed manner whether their team is ahead or behind. This unwavering focus enables them to perform at their best regardless of the circumstances on the ice.

Pro Tip From Coach Austin:
"Create a post goal routine that is the same for a goal against and a goal for. This can help you begin to control your emotions and react the same way in both scenarios...the sign of a mentally tough athlete!"

Do We Have A Problem?
To help you build consistent reactions regardless of outcome, one technique I love is the "Do we have a problem?" question. Many of the mistakes we make on the ice, including those resulting in goals, are often not as catastrophic as they may initially appear. Even a misdirected pass to the opposing team ultimately has minimal impact on your overall career and long-term goals. Yet, in the heat of the moment, we tend to react as though they do. At such times, it's invaluable to pause and ask yourself, "Do we have a problem?" More

often than not, the answer is a resounding "NO." These mistakes only escalate into problems if you allow them to. When you remind yourself that there is, in fact, no problem, you can release the tension of the moment and refocus your attention on the task at hand, which still demands your performance. Even a critical error that ends a game isn't a definitive problem because you understand that there will be another opportunity for redemption.

The best athletes in the world understand that mistakes are part of the process, which is why they persist after a failed play, pass, or game. They don't perceive it as a problem; instead, they recognize it as an opportunity for further improvement and growth, and they know there is still a job to take care of.

The Way You React Says More About You Than the Situation...
You're on the ice, Game 1 of a big tournament. It's a tie game with one minute left, and the crowd is roaring. You've had a great game so far, only giving up one goal on 30 shots. In the last 20 seconds, a quick one timer comes from the slot, the puck whizzes past your blocker, finding the back of the net. The crowd erupts, disappointment washes over you, and frustration threatens to consume your thoughts.

In the locker room after the game, a forward on your team lashes out at you, criticizing your performance in front of the entire team. You know you played well, that mistakes and goals happen. How do you react in this moment? Do you allow their words to deflate your confidence going into Game 2, letting anger and frustration take hold? Or do you choose to remain composed, recognizing that their behavior and words say more about them than it does about you?

You see, it's easy to blame external factors when things don't go our way. We might point fingers at teammates for missed opportunities or curse our luck for an unlucky bounce. But the truth is, our reactions reveal more about our character and mindset than they do about the circumstances we find ourselves in.

Consider the mindset of a mentally tough athlete. They understand that mistakes are an inevitable part of the game. They don't dwell on what went wrong; instead, they focus on what they can control—their response. Rather than succumbing to frustration or self-doubt, they use setbacks as fuel for growth and improvement. Your teammate in the above scenario isn't mentally tough, they are mentally soft, thinking that lashing out at you will make them feel better about their performance.

In this scenario, your reaction speaks volumes about your character and mental toughness. It's easy to let emotions run wild and lash out in return, but true strength lies in maintaining composure and rising above negativity. By responding with grace and resilience, you demonstrate your ability to navigate challenging situations with poise and maturity. All you can control is yourself.

Now, let's apply this principle to the realm of sports and mental toughness. In the high-pressure environment of competitive athletics, adversity is inevitable. Whether it's a missed shot, a costly error, or criticism from teammates or coaches, how you react in these moments can make all the difference in your performance and overall success moving forward. Take, for example, the legendary goaltender who lets in a game-winning goal. In the face of defeat, they don't hang their head in despair or blame their teammates. Instead, they rise to the occasion, channeling their resilience and determination into preparation for the next game. They understand that true strength lies not in avoiding failure, but in how we respond to it.

Similarly, when faced with adversity from teammates or opponents, mentally tough athletes maintain their composure and stay focused on their goals. Instead of getting caught up in drama or negativity, they channel their energy into productive actions, such as pushing themselves harder in practice or supporting their teammates on and off the ice or field. They focus on everything they can control, and none of what they can't.

Mental toughness is the ultimate equalizer. It's what separates the good from the great, the champions from the contenders. It's the ability to stay composed under pressure, to
bounce back from setbacks, and to maintain focus amidst chaos. And just like in the game of hockey, life is full of unexpected challenges and obstacles. How we react to these challenges—whether on the ice or in our daily lives—defines who we are and if we have success.

The next time you find yourself facing adversity, whatever that adversity is (a bad game, cruel coach, getting cut from a team, pulled in a game, a bad grade in school), remember: it's not the situation that determines your fate, but how you choose to react to it. It's in these moments that we ask ourselves, "What is within my control?". Usually, the only controllable we have is our attitude and how we will react. Do we fall apart mentally, or do we rise above?

Horses Race With Blinders On
Have you ever watched a horse race? You might have noticed something peculiar about the horses—they wear blinders on the outer sides of their heads around their eyes. These small, seemingly insignificant pieces of equipment serve a crucial purpose: they restrict the horse's field of vision, allowing them to focus solely on

what lies ahead, blocking out distractions and external stimuli.

Blinders

Now, let's apply this concept to the realm of sports and goaltending. As an athlete, you face a myriad of distractions on, and off, the ice—crowds cheering, opponents taunting, and the pressure to perform at your best. In the midst of chaos, maintaining focus becomes paramount to your success.

Just like horses wearing blinders, mental toughness in athletes involves the ability to block out distractions and stay laser-focused on the task at hand. You want to have a mindset of unwavering determination and resilience, regardless of the circumstances around you, or, even the internal chatter in your head.

It's important to understand that mental toughness is not about being impervious to pressure or never having feelings of doubt—it's about acknowledging those feelings and choosing to persevere despite them. When you're mentally tough, you recognize that obstacles and setbacks are a natural part of the game, but they don't define your performance or your worth as an athlete.

The 'blinders' metaphor can help you fix something else as well, something you do every day, sometimes without even realizing it, and it's called "creating comparisons".

In the world of sports, (and let's face it, the age of social media) it's easy to fall into the trap of comparing yourself to others. Whether it's measuring your performance against that of your teammates or comparing your stats to those of rival goaltenders, the urge to gauge your worth based on external benchmarks can be strong. But here's the thing: comparing yourself to others is like taking off a horse's blinders in the middle of a race. It distracts you from the task at hand and undermines your mental focus. Just as a horse races with blinders on to block out distractions, you too must stay focused on your own journey and goals, and fight the urge to look left and right around every bend.

Every person is on their own unique path, facing their own challenges and obstacles. What works for one goaltender may not work for another, and that's okay. The path to college hockey for one athlete will be totally different then it is for another, I can attest to that. Embrace your individuality and focus on maximizing your own potential on your current path, rather than constantly measuring yourself against others. One phrase I love to remind my athletes of is "Don't compare your Chapter 1 to their Chapter 50". Someone else's life, career, or path, is in a totally different book on a totally different shelf in the library. It is silly to compare our chapters to theirs. Being mentally tough is understanding that you can, and will, write your own story, with it's own chapters, that is totally unique to you.

Instead of comparing yourself to your peers, use them as motivation to push yourself further. Celebrate their successes and learn from their achievements, but never let your peers or competition dictate your own worth or definition of your goals. By staying in your lane and keeping your blinders on, you can maintain unwavering focus on your own journey, blocking out distractions and external pressures. Trust in your abilities, believe in your potential, and keep your eyes fixed firmly on the next step in front of YOU. In the end, it's not about how you stack up against others—it's about how you measure up to who you were yesterday.

The comparison fallacy, also known as the comparison trap, is the killer of many dreams, and leads to "Imposter Syndrome"; the feeling that everyone but you is deserving of success. Because of this, comparisons are one of the biggest reasons athletes struggle to grow mental toughness and the reason many stop pursuing their dreams. The comparison trap doesn't allow for a powerful mindset like mental toughness to exist within it's fallacy. While you are working to grow your mental strength, begin by identifying areas where you are falling into the comparison trap, and start to turn them off.

Four ways that you can break free from comparisons:
1. **Focus on Personal Progress:** Instead of comparing save percentages or goals allowed with other goalies, focus on your own progress and improvement. Set personal goals for each practice session or game and track your own development over time. Celebrate your achievements and milestones, regardless of how they compare to others.
2. **Embrace Individuality:** Recognize that each goalie has their own unique strengths, weaknesses, and playing style. Embrace your individuality and focus on maximizing your own potential rather than trying to emulate or compete with other goalies. Celebrate what makes you unique and capitalize on your strengths to enhance your performance.
3. **Practice Gratitude:** Cultivate a mindset of gratitude for the opportunities and experiences you have as a goalie. Instead of dwelling on what others may have or achieve, focus on appreciating your own journey and the support you receive from teammates, coaches, and fans. Gratitude can help shift your perspective away from comparison and towards fulfillment and contentment with your own path.
4. **Compete Against Yourself:** Be better than no one, except who you were yesterday.

CHAPTER 4

YOUR 3 CONTROLLABLES

One of the most powerful lessons an athlete can learn is how limited their control is over everything around them. In fact, in any given situation, life or sports, there are only three things you have control over.

Your 3 Controllables are your **Attitude**, **Effort**, and **Preparation**. That's it. Within any given situation, these are the only aspects you can influence directly. Recognizing and embracing these controllables is pivotal in the development of mental toughness. By understanding that these three factors, and these three only, are within your power to shape and mold, you can cultivate resilience, determination, and a proactive approach to challenges.

In order to grow mentally tough, its first crucial to recognize that the majority of variables are outside of our direct control. As goaltenders, we face a myriad of unpredictable factors—from the skill level of our opponents to the conditions of the ice—that can significantly impact the outcome of a game. Reflecting on this reality can be daunting, but it's also a fundamental aspect of developing mental toughness and resilience. If you constantly worry or panic about things you have no control over, you will feel helpless, angry, and frustrated about your current state. Consider individuals who consistently worry about the actions of others rather than focusing on themselves. Instead of prioritizing self-awareness and personal growth, they become absorbed in someone else's narrative. An athlete who fixates on the referees' calls instead of concentrating on their own contributions to the game, tends to become engulfed in feelings of anger and frustration. This distraction from their own performance can lead to missed opportunities for personal growth and improvement. Once you accept that most things are beyond your control, you can start directing your attention to what you can control within yourself.

Consider a scenario where you're preparing to play in a crucial playoff game. You've been training all season, prepared pre game like normal, and visualized how you want the game to go. However, once the puck drops, you quickly realize that the game is unfolding in ways you hadn't anticipated. Your team is nervous and shaky, the opposing team's offense takes advantage, the puck takes unexpected bounces, and your own teammates get unlucky penalty calls against them. In this moment, it becomes abundantly clear that the vast majority of factors influencing the game are beyond your control.

As a goaltender, it's easy to feel overwhelmed by the sheer number of variables that lie outside of your sphere of influence. The performance of your teammates, the decisions of the referees, and even the actions of the opposing players are all elements that you cannot directly manipulate. Instead of becoming fixated on factors beyond your control, it's essential to shift your focus to what you can influence—your attitude, effort, and preparation. While you may not be able to dictate the outcome of the game or control the actions of others, you have the power to control how you respond to adversity, the level of effort you exert on the ice, and the degree of preparation you bring to each game.

Understanding this truth can cultivate a calm mindset. You've streamlined your approach to the game and simplified your mindset. Instead of fretting over numerous external factors, you now have just three aspects that require your attention! It's a shift from juggling a multitude of concerns to concentrating on a concise set of priorities. A simple and focused mind is a mentally tough one. The more you worry about things you can't control, the less focused you'll be on the task at hand. Does your role change if the game is 0-0 or 11-0? Does it change if the referee makes a call against your team, or if the opposing player chirps you? Whether you're facing a 5-on-3 penalty kill or a breakaway, your objective remains unchanged: stop the puck. Once you simplify your role, and focus only on what controllables you have, you will be mentally tough and nothing the game, season, or life throws at you will phase you. Don't let the situations or the people around you change how you play, how you react, or who you are.

> **📌 Pro Tip From Coach Austin:**
> *"In the fast-paced chaos of the game, you must anchor themselves in what they can control. Remind yourself often. Whether it's a 0-0 tie or a blowout, your role remains consistent: stop the puck. What other areas of your life do you catch yourself worrying in? Boil down your controllables in those moments to our 3: Attitude, Effort, Preparation."*

At the core of mental toughness lies a profound sense of empowerment—a belief that you have the power to shape your own destiny. By focusing on your controllables—your attitude, effort, and preparation—you reclaim control over your performance and outcomes.

Attitude

Our attitude, in particular, can be our greatest asset in the face of adversity. Your career is no stranger to adversity. From the heartbreak of giving up a crucial goal to the frustration of being pulled from a game, you've faced numerous challenges that have tested your resolve and resilience. However, in the face of these obstacles, there's one thing that can make all the difference: your response, a.k.a your attitude.

The attitude you bring to the ice profoundly impacts your performance and mindset. A negative outlook can draw in more challenges, while a positive one equips you to face adversity with resilience, minimizing its impact on your game

In athletics, adversity is inevitable. As goalies, it could be in the form of giving up a goal, getting pulled from a game, or facing disagreements with our coach. No matter what phase of our career we're in, we are constantly being tested in ways we never imagined. However, it's our attitude in these moments that truly defines us. Instead of letting negativity consume us, we can choose to approach each challenge with an understanding of what we can control first. By focusing on what we can control, in particular, our attitude, we can turn setbacks into opportunities for growth and learning.

Opportunity or Obligation?

When I think of having a great attitude, Marc-Andre Fleury always comes to mind. Consistently seen with a smile, he's clearly relishing every moment. A valuable lesson from Marc-Andre is that regardless of the circumstance, there's always room for growth and learning, beginning with our attitude.

Imagine you are face to face with a 5-on-3 penalty kill, the opposing team pulls their goalie, and it's 6-on-3 with just a minute left in regulation. Your team is clinging to a one-goal lead. In these critical moments, elite goaltenders see the challenge as an opportunity to shine. Are they nervous? Of course, but elite goaltenders don't succumb to the "what if" whispers in their minds. Instead, they confront the challenge head-on, viewing it as an opportunity to secure victory despite the odds against them. This is attitude in a nut shell. A fearful goaltender will allow nerves to consume them, and begin preparing for a tie game before it even happens. They'll blame the refs for the call, their team for the penalties, themselves for feeling this way. Relax. Let go of that defense mechanism. Shift your mindset to one of opportunity. You can't control penalty calls or a 6-on-3 situation, but you can control your attitude and the effort you put into finishing the game strong.

An easy way to adjust our attitude is to opt for gratitude over negativity. Take the previous example. An elite goalie is going to find "privilege in the pressure". To maintain focus and shut down opponents, they embrace the opportunity to excel in high-intensity moments. Conversely, a goalie struggling with mental toughness may succumb to fear, adopting a "Why is this happening to me?" mindset. Which one sounds more powerful to you?

The more we choose a grateful mindset, the easier adopting a productive attitude on the ice is going to be. When we are grateful, we erase the negative thoughts that hold us back. If you ever find yourself thinking, "this is happening TO me", change the script to "this is happening FOR me". That small shift is a powerful way to affirm that no matter what happens in life or on the ice, you are going to rise above it. We'll talk more about this later.

Expressing gratitude holds immense power in our lives. If there's one change you can implement today, let it be embracing gratitude. Consider starting your day by expressing gratitude for the opportunities and blessings in your life. By focusing on what you're thankful for, you shift your mindset to one of abundance and positivity. This positive energy can attract more opportunities and success your way, as you approach each day with a mindset of gratitude and openness. You'll notice the change on the ice as well, and find yourself having more fun, and not relying on external factors to determine your feeling of success in the crease.

Effort

"Hard work beats talent when talent doesn't work hard"

You've heard that quote from Tim Notke, seen it on poster, maybe it's even the lock screen on your phone. I love Tim's phrase, and I've also made my own version:

"Mental toughness beats talent when talent is soft".

Both quotes are powerful reminders that being talented isn't enough. It may get you started, but effort and mental toughness will keep you going. Effort is more than just physical exertion—it's a mindset. It's the unwavering commitment to giving 100% in every practice, every game, and every situation, regardless of the outcome. As goaltenders, our effort is one of our most potent weapons against adversity and our greatest catalyst for growth. Effort is the cornerstone of mental toughness—it's what enables us to persevere when the going gets tough, to push through fatigue and discomfort, and to rise above adversity.

When coupled with the attitude controllable, effort separates us from the pack and is also the key to personal growth and development as an athlete. It's what enables us to push past our limits and break through barriers we didn't even think were possible to break! It could be spending extra time on the ice, working with a coach to refine our technique, or studying game film to identify areas for improvement, our effort is what propels us forward.

A productive attitude and 110% effort is an athlete to be reckoned with, a player a coach on any team wants to have. Without a productive attitude, your effort will be deflected to areas that won't be beneficial to you. Too much effort will be given to things outside your control, or thoughts that hinder, rather than help. Effort that is channeled the right way, will result in you growing substantially faster than your counterparts. Athletes that channel effort the right way are our elite athletes, and elite athletes grasp that perfection isn't feasible for every repetition or game outcome. However, they remain unfazed by setbacks because they've committed to maintaining consistent effort regardless of external variables each day.

> **📌 Pro Tip From Coach Austin:**
> *"Don't allow someone to remind you to give effort. Coaches shouldn't have to be on your case about showing up and putting in the work day in and day out".*

Preparation

Preparation is our third and final controllable and rounds out the trio. Preparation is a controllable because we alone have power over it. Athletes have control over preparation because it is a deliberate and intentional action that we can choose to prioritize and execute. Unlike external factors such as ice conditions or the decisions of referees, preparation is entirely within the athlete's sphere of influence. It encompasses a wide range of activities, including training, conditioning, mental rehearsal, studying opponents, and developing game plans. We have the autonomy to decide how much time and effort we dedicate to each aspect of preparation, making it a controllable variable in our performance. Ultimately, the level of preparation will directly impact our readiness, confidence, and ability to perform at our best, making it a critical factor in our success on and off the ice.

Preparation can range from a pregame routine, gameday meal, mental rehearsal, visualization, and dynamic warmups. Preparation is often unique to the individual and can be different in different situations. At face value, it may seem as though preparation can be affected by external forces, but in reality, it cannot. I'll explain.

Imagine for a second you are on the way to your game. If you drive yourself, imagine you hit traffic, If you are on a team bus, imagine the bus driver takes the wrong exit (happened to me all the time!). If your parents drive you, imagine that they are late leaving the house. Whatever the reasoning, you are running extremely late. You know that by the time you get to the rink you'll have 20 minutes before warmups start and not the usual one to two hours.

In this situation you may think, "My game day preparation is completely disrupted, I am not in control anymore". And while you may not dictate the timing of your arrival at the rink, you still retain full control over your preparation. Recognizing that warm-up time is limited, you adjust your approach accordingly. Instead of succumbing to anxiety, you pivot your focus towards mental rehearsal and visualization exercises, even conducting them during your commute on the car or bus. Rather than allowing external circumstances to dictate your mindset, you affirm your resilience and determination. You remind yourself that a delay does not alter your identity as a player on the ice. Despite the less-than-ideal circumstances, you assert your control over what remains within your grasp: your preparation. Upon reaching the rink, you swiftly drop your bag in the locker room and engage in a brief two-and-a-half-minute static stretching routine before suiting up. While the situation may not be ideal, you understand that certain factors were beyond your control. Nevertheless, you take charge of the elements still within your reach: your readiness and mindset.

With this approach, a game that could have been filled with anxiety due to the rushing around and late arrival, is now a stage for you to showcase your mental toughness. All those factors outside your control had no affect on you. You are mentally tough!

Now that you are familiar with our three controllables, let's go through our list of non-controllables again. While you read through the list think of your three controllables: Attitude, Effort, and Preparation. On each list item recognize how the external factor has not affected any of your three controllables:
- A bad call by the referee
- Your teammate's opinion
- The skill level of your team

- The skill level of the team you are playing against
- The people in the crowd
- Decisions your friends make
- Coach's decision on who's playing
- Getting pulled in a game
- Getting cut from a team
- The rink your playing at

The three controllables offer checks and balances for each other as well. On days when you're feeling down, effort can boost your attitude. Times when preparation is difficult, attitude and effort will carry you. In the rare occasions that effort lacks, attitude and preparation can keep you going. Release the grip on factors beyond your influence as you embrace the three controllables and grow mentally tough.

CHAPTER 5

I EMBRACE THE UNCERTAINTY

One of my favorite personal affirmations is, "I am embrace the uncertainty". It's a powerful affirmation for every aspect of your life, but it's also is a mental toughness building block, and I had to include it in this book.

As we learned in the last chapter, it's important to prepare and plan, but it's equally as important to be flexible and have the ability to pivot quickly when things don't go as planned. Being adaptable is a sign of a truly mentally tough athlete because they won't allow themselves to be thrown off by changes in schedule, unexpected situations, bad calls, changes in lineups, or events not panning out as expected or wanted. Conversely, a mentally fragile athlete, impacted negatively by such changes, will lose their footing and struggle to adapt and deliver their best performance.

Embracing uncertainty is crucial in building mental toughness because it cultivates resilience and adaptability. In the face of uncertainty, individuals are often forced to confront their fears and step outside their comfort zones. The process fosters the development of coping mechanisms, problem-solving skills, and emotional regulation—all of which are essential components of mental toughness. For athletes, embracing uncertainty helps us remain calm and composed in unpredictable situations, allowing us to stay focused on goals and navigate challenges with confidence and determination. In today's world, one undeniable truth is unpredictability—anything can happen. Therefore, being ill-equipped to handle setbacks and uncertainty isn't really an option. Reality is full of unexpected twists, making it vital to be able to navigate these changes without losing sight of yourself, your ambitions, and your goals. Ultimately, by embracing uncertainty, we can learn to thrive in dynamic environments, turning adversity into opportunity and setbacks into stepping stones for growth.

If you recognize that you are a person who struggles with embracing the uncertainty, start training your mindset to help make this process easier. Begin first by challenging your negative thoughts and anxiety surrounding uncertainty. Practice challenging your thoughts by asking questions like, "What evidence do I have that this outcome will be negative?" or "What are alternative, more positive outcomes?" By reframing your perspective and focusing on the potential for positive outcomes, you will reduce anxiety and increase your willingness to embrace uncertainty. You must first accept that uncertainty will happen no matter what, and then ask yourself, "Would I rather fight reality and be miserable, or embrace it and take control?".

Embracing mental toughness means being adaptable. When you

acknowledge that personal control is confined to your Attitude, Effort, and Preparation, uncertainty loses its grip on you. You cease fretting over situations not unfolding as planned because you understand focusing on what you can control will yield positive adaptations in your favor.

Apply R.A.P.

To assist you in embracing uncertainty, I've devised the acronym R.A.P: Reality, Acceptance, Perception. R.A.P. serves as a potent reminder that resisting reality only leads to further anguish and mental fatigue. Instead, when faced with an unexpected situation, strive to embrace ACCEPTance of your reality. Once you've embraced what's before you and the circumstances you find yourself in, only then can you begin to shift your perception of it. Two individuals could encounter the same scenario, yet one may perceive it positively while the other negatively. Your perception and acceptance of your surroundings are paramount. Whether you view the glass as half full or half empty is secondary to making the most of what you have.

Resisting reality is futile; the past cannot be changed, only the present. Embracing the reality you're confronted with enables you to direct your energy and efforts toward the aspects you can presently control, paving the way for the changes you wish to enact.

📌 Pro Tip From Coach Austin:

"Try this affirmation out daily: When you wake up recite 'I Embrace the Uncertainty'.
Before games, or stressful moments, recite it again and feel noticeably calmer."

CHAPTER 6

MOUNTAINS TO MOLEHILLS

Adversity is an unavoidable aspect of goaltending. From facing relentless offensive attacks to navigating the intense pressure of high-stakes matchups, goaltending requires athletes to possess resilience and determination to thrive.

Being able to overcome adversity is similar to our Chapter 2 discussion of resilience, and is the final boss in growing your mental toughness. The difference between overcoming adversity and developing resilience lies in their focus and scope:

Adversity: Overcoming adversity specifically refers to the action of triumphing over specific challenges or difficult circumstances. It involves successfully navigating through obstacles, setbacks, or hardships and emerging on the other side with strength, growth, and success. This concept highlights the outcome of facing and conquering adversity, emphasizing the ability to prevail despite difficult circumstances.

Resilience: On the other hand, developing resilience is a broader and ongoing process that involves building the capacity to withstand, adapt to, and bounce back from various challenges, not just specific adversities. Resilience is more about the underlying traits, skills, and mindset that enable individuals to effectively cope with adversity over the long term. It encompasses the ability to maintain mental and emotional well-being in the face of adversity, as well as the capacity to learn and grow from challenging experiences.

While overcoming adversity focuses on successfully conquering specific challenges, developing resilience involves cultivating the skills, mindset, and behaviors that enable individuals to navigate adversity more effectively in general.

Mastering resilience techniques, as discussed in Chapter 2, is crucial for overcoming adversity. Your goal is to reach a point in your career where challenges carry equal weight, regardless of their appearance. For instance, a mentally tough goalie will be able to view giving up a goal the same way they view getting cut or traded by a team. While the situations are vastly different in impact, a mentally strong goalie overcomes both without letting external appearances magnify the adversity; i.e. they tackle getting cut with the same mindset they tackle conceding a goal. Visualize the power of your mindset if mountains were mere molehills. The ebbs and flows of emotions are a much smaller spread. That's true mental toughness.

Adversity takes many forms. Short and long term injuries, negative family situations impacting your game, academic hardships, being traded or cut, entering a new organization...adversity is everywhere and how resilient you are to it and how you respond is everything.

Step back and ask yourself now, am I resilient to and adaptative to challenges? Do I bounce back? Do I view larger forms of adversity the same way I view minor ones? How can I utilize my three controllables to overcome adversity and not turn molehills into mountains?

Pro Tip From Coach Austin:
"The difference in succumbing to adversity versus overcoming adversity, can be found in the two main types of mindsets: the Fixed Mindset and the Growth Mindset. Let's talk about these next."

CHAPTER 7

THE 2 STATES OF BEING

Are you the victim, or are you empowered? We've spoken about the growth mindset a few times already, but we can't fully understand the growth mindset without understanding the Mr. Hyde to its Dr. Jekyll: the fixed mindset. While the growth mindset emphasizes continual growth and advancement, even in the face of challenges, the fixed mindset is characterized by stagnation, maintaining the status quo, or even regression, as stagnation leads to decline. Often termed the victim mindset, the fixed mindset revolves around feelings of powerlessness and a tendency to blame external factors for one's circumstances. Individuals with a fixed mindset frequently find themselves asking, "Why is this happening to me?" instead of seeking opportunities for growth and improvement.

This is happening TO me or this is happening FOR me
Individuals with a growth mindset possess the ability to perceive the

world unfolding before them. Even amidst significant challenges, mentally tough athletes with a growth mindset can discern the constructive potential within their circumstances. Instead of perceiving adversity as the world conspiring against them, they regard it as an opportunity to harness the world's potential. The key distinction between individuals with a fixed mindset and those with a growth mindset lies in the questions they ask themselves. Those with a victim mindset believe that negative occurrences are imposed upon them by external forces, blaming these factors for their circumstances. Conversely, individuals with a growth mindset confront external challenges directly and focus inwardly on their controllables to determine actionable changes. They ask themselves empowering questions, reframing adversity as an opportunity for personal growth and development.

We all struggle with the victim mindset from time to time. However, if you catch yourself in that mindset often during the day, begin shifting the narrative by altering the questions you pose to yourself and the internal dialogue you engage in. When confronted with a challenging situation or adversity, challenge yourself to reframe your perspective. Rather than asking, "**Why** is this happening?" prompt yourself with, "**How** can I transform this into an opportunity?" This shift in mindset can lead to profound changes in how you approach and overcome obstacles.

For a mentally tough athlete, recognizing and overcoming the victim mindset is essential for maintaining peak performance. When faced with adversity, such as a string of losses or a career-threatening injury, they understand the importance of reframing their perspective. Instead of succumbing to self-pity or blaming external factors, they proactively seek ways to turn challenges into opportunities for growth.

A mentally tough athlete consciously alters their internal dialogue. When up against adversity, rather than asking, "Why is this happening to me?" they pivot to a more empowering question: "How can I use this experience to become stronger and more resilient?" By adopting this mindset shift, they reclaim control over their circumstances and focus their energy on productive solutions. It reflects back to embracing the uncertainty and not fighting our reality. This change in perspective allows a mentally tough athlete to approach adversity with resilience and determination. They understand that setbacks are temporary and view them as stepping stones on the path to success. Through self-reflection and a commitment to personal growth, they transform adversity into fuel for motivation, pushing themselves to new heights of achievement both on and off the ice, field, or court.

In your everyday life, begin to take note of your thoughts when you have them. Ask yourself, am I treating my circumstance like I am a victim, or am I viewing it through a lens of growth and opportunity? Am I blaming my parents, my coaches, my teammates, the refs, politics in my organization, or other factors for my circumstance? Or, am I taking the circumstance for what it is, embracing the uncertainty, and only looking at what I have in my control?

If you are struggling with a victim mindset holding you back, begin to alter it by questioning assumptions and beliefs that reinforce your fixed mindset. Replace negative self-talk with positive and empowering language, to shift your mindset and bolster confidence. For example, instead of thinking, "I'm not good enough," reframe your thoughts to say, "I am capable of overcoming challenges and improving with practice" or, "Day by day in everyway I am getting better" or, "I am better than I was yesterday".

To snap out of victim mentality and embrace one of growth and mental toughness, you must also embrace failure as a learning opportunity. As we've discussed, failure is an inevitable part of the athletic journey, but it doesn't have to be viewed as a reflection of your abilities. One goal against doesn't define your overall skill as a goaltender. You can shift your perspective on failure by embracing it as a natural part of the learning process. Instead of dwelling on mistakes or setbacks, let's extract valuable lessons and insights from each experience. For example, rather than seeing a missed shot as a personal failure, view it as an opportunity to practice your game and improve skill sets you need to focus on.

Lastly, grow out of that victim mindset by focusing on our three controllables instead of being fixated on outcomes. In a results-driven culture, it's easy for us to become obsessed with outcomes and results. However, prioritizing effort and growth over outcomes will help you cultivate a growth mindset. Set process-oriented goals focused on continuous improvement rather than fixed notions of success or failure. All-or-nothing thinking is dangerous, because it leaves no room for growth! By celebrating progress, regardless of the outcome, we can reinforce the idea that effort and perseverance are key determinants of success. This isn't "everyone gets a participation trophy", rather, it's the personal celebration of growth through the process. Instead of solely fixating on winning a game, establish objectives geared towards enhancing skills, giving 100%, and bolstering resilience. This approach ensures that we maintain mental toughness throughout the game, regardless of the score.

CHAPTER 8

ACHIEVING VICTORY WITH A WINNING MINDSET

Mental toughness wouldn't be complete without emphasizing the importance of cultivating a winning mindset. A winning mindset isn't only about winning games; it's about approaching every challenge with positivity, determination, and unwavering belief in oneself. Take these final thoughts into your next practice. Mental toughness isn't born overnight, but these final three points are a great way to grow the process and help you develop your mindset each and every day.

Positive Self-Talk and Belief in Yourself
Positive self-talk and self-belief are fundamental pillars of a winning mindset. Athletes who cultivate a habit of positive self-talk maintain an inner dialogue that uplifts and motivates them, even in the face of adversity. By affirming their abilities and visualizing success, athletes bolster their confidence and resilience. Believing in oneself is the foundation upon which all other aspects of mental toughness are

built, laying the groundwork for achievement and success. Recite affirmations, repeat phrases to yourself in your head, remind yourself each day why you are great. When you truly believe in your power, no adversity can get you down.

Start with these affirmations:
- I am a great goalie
- I am confident
- I am mentally tough
- I embrace the uncertainty
- Day by day, everyway, I'm getting better and better
- I embrace my controllables
- I am strong
- I am present
- I am enough and have always been enough

A Mindset of Determination and Perseverance
Determination and perseverance are essential qualities for athletes striving to cultivate a winning mindset. In the face of obstacles and setbacks, it's crucial to maintain a steadfast commitment to one's goals and aspirations. Challenges are inevitable, but temporary, and elite athletes approach them with a spirit of resilience and perseverance. They view setbacks as opportunities for growth and remain unwavering in their pursuit of excellence. Embrace the uncertainty!

Building Confidence Through Preparation and Practice
Confidence is the bedrock of a winning mindset, and it is cultivated through diligent preparation and practice. Athletes who dedicate themselves to honing their skills, refining their techniques, and mastering their craft instill a sense of confidence that permeates

every aspect of their performance. By immersing themselves in the process of preparation and practice, elite athletes build a reservoir of self-assurance that enables them to perform at their best when it matters most. Practice is physically for honing skills, but mentally it's going to help you feel confident in those skills. Go above and beyond at your practices and feel your mind develop into one of toughness.

Remind yourself often that a winning mindset is not just about winning game. In order to have one, you must embrace challenges with resilience, positivity, and unwavering determination. Allow yourself to set the stage for triumph and achievement in every endeavor. When you view everything as a stepping stone in your growth, challenges become fun, adversity becomes no big deal, and anxieties are easier to let go of.

> **Pro Tip From Coach Austin:**
> *"We all want to win, but sometimes factors contributing to that W are out of our control. It's important to remember that it's not about the wins and losses, it's about how you play the game. Having this mentality can help you stay mentally strong even in the face of a tough opponent, poor team play, or situations that result in difficult performances."*

> **Pro Tip From Coach Austin:**
> *"Starting with the phrases on page 42, create 1 or 2 in-game phrases that you can repeat in your head that will reinforce positive self talk or present moment focus. Mine are "I am present" and I am where I am supposed to be."*

CHAPTER 9

SOLIDIFYING YOUR FOUNDATION

It's clear that mental toughness and resilience are qualities indispensable for success both on and off the ice. Throughout this guide, we've delved into the significance of mental toughness in sports performance, understanding resilience, and conquering adversity. We've also learned practical techniques for enhancing mental toughness, including psychological skills training, goal-setting, and visualization exercises.

Yet, mental toughness transcends mere athletic achievement; it's about approaching challenges with unwavering determination, perseverance, and self-belief. By dialing our focus on our controllables and embracing the uncertainty around us, we can navigate the pressures of our position with confidence.

As you transition from the rink to the broader world, I urge you to embody these principles. Embrace mental toughness in all aspects of your life—whether facing formidable opponents, rebounding from setbacks, or pursuing your aspirations. With the right mindset and unwavering resolve, you possess the ability to overcome any obstacle in your path.

I want to encourage you to take what you've learned here and put it into practice. Don't just read it and forget about it. Take action and start implementing these techniques in your training and in your games. Building mental toughness is a journey, and it takes time and effort. There will be ups and downs along the way, but don't get discouraged. Remember, control of the world around you is not possible, only control of yourself is. Don't lose the control of your mind and body, and shift your focus to the small things you can do each day to maintain control over yourself, your choices, and your path. When you start to find yourself looking left and right, remember the horses with blinders on, and embody that mentally, knowing that glancing at someone else's path will just throw you off yours.

You are more powerful than you can imagine, and tougher than you know. Once you accept this, mental toughness will be your way of life, both on and off the ice.

Above all, remember to have fun! Hockey is a game, and it's meant to be enjoyed. Don't put too much pressure on yourself.

Good luck on your journey!

FURTHER RESOURCES

Mental Skills Training for Goaltenders:

thementalgoalie.thinkific.com

A Goaltender's Guide to Building Confidence in the Crease:

https://a.co/d/2PyX8fk

5 Books Goalies Must Read:

https://thementalgoalieschool.com/top-5-books-all-hockey-goalies-must-read/

In Season Goalie Journal:

https://thementalgoalieschool.com/stat-tracking-journal

Made in the USA
Columbia, SC
06 January 2025